The Poetry of Francis Beaumont

Francis Beaumont was born in 1584 near the small Leicestershire village of Thringstone. Unfortunately precise records of much of his short life do not exist.

The first date we can give for his education is at age 13 when he begins at Broadgates Hall (now Pembroke College, Oxford). Sadly, his father died the following year, 1598. Beaumont left university without a degree and entered the Inner Temple in London in 1600. A career choice of Law taken previously by his father.

The information to hand is confident that Beaumont's career in law was short-lived. He was quickly attracted to the theatre and soon became first an admirer and then a student of poet and playwright Ben Jonson. Jonson at this time was a cultural behemoth; very talented and a life full of volatility that included frequent brushes with the authorities.

Beaumont's first work was Salmacis and Hermaphroditus, it debuted in 1602.

By 1605, Beaumont had written commendatory verses to Volpone one of Ben Jonson's masterpieces.

His solo playwriting career was limited. Apart from his poetry there were only two; The Knight of the Burning Pestle was first performed by the Children of the Blackfriars company in 1607. The audience however was distinctly unimpressed.

The Masque of the Gentlemen of Grays-Inne and the Inner-Temple was written for part of the wedding festivities for the Princess Elizabeth, daughter of King James I and Frederick V, Elector Palatine. It was performed on 20 February 1613 in the Banqueting House at Whitehall Palace.

By that point his collaboration with John Fletcher, which was to cover approximately 15 plays together with further works later revised by Philip Massinger, was about to end after his stroke and death later that year.

That collaboration is seen as one of the most significant and fruitful of the English theatre.

Index of Contents

The Author to the Reader

I sing the fortune of a luckless pair,
Whose spotless souls now in one body be;
For beauty still is Prodromus to care,
Crost by the sad stars of nativity:
And of the strange enchantment of a well,
Given by the Gods, my sportive muse doth write,
Which sweet-lipp'd Ovid long ago did tell,
Wherein who bathes, straight turns Hermaphrodite:
I hope my poem is so lively writ,
That thou wilt turn half-mad with reading it.

Salmacis and Hermaphroditus

My wanton lines doe treate of amorous loue,
Such as would bow the hearts of gods aboue:
Then Venus, thou great Citherean Queene,
That hourely tript on the Idalian greene,
Thou laughing Erycina, daygne to see
The verses wholly consecrate to thee;
Temper them so within thy Paphian shrine,
That euery Louers eye may melt a line;
Commaund the god of Loue that little King,
To giue each verse a sleight touch with his wing,
That as I write, one line may draw the tother,

And euery word skip nimbly o're another.
There was a louely boy the Nymphs had kept,
That on the Idane mountains oft had slept,
Begot and borne by powers that dwelt aboue,
By learned Mercury of the Queene of loue:
A face he had that shew'd his parents fame,
And from them both conioynd, he drew his name:
So wondrous fayre he was that (as they say)
Diana being hunting on a day,
Shee saw the boy vpon a greene banke lay him,
And there the virgin-huntresse meant to slay him,
Because no Nymphes did now pursue the chase:
For all were strooke blind with the wanton's face.
But when that beauteous face Diana saw,
Her armes were nummed, & shee could not draw;
Yet she did striue to shoot, but all in vaine,
Shee bent her bow, and loos'd it streight againe.
Then she began to chide her wanton eye,
And fayne would shoot, but durst not see him die,
She turnd and shot, and did of purpose misse him,
Shee turnd againe, and did of purpose kisse him.
Then the boy ran: for (some say) had he stayd,
Diana had no longer bene a mayd.
Phoebus so doted on this rosiat face,
That he hath oft stole closely from his place,
When he did lie by fayre Leucothoes side,
To dally with him in the vales of Ide:
And euer since this louely boy did die,
Phoebus each day about the world doth flie,
And on the earth he seekes him all the day,
And euery night he seekes him in the sea:
His cheeke was sanguine, and his lip as red
As are the blushing leaues of the Rose spred:
And I haue heard, that till this boy was borne,
Rose grew white vpon the virgin thorne,
Till one day walking to a pleasant spring,
To heare how cunningly the birds could sing,
Laying him downe vpon a flowry bed,
The Roses blush'd and turn'd themselues to red.
The Rose that blush'd not, for his great offence,
The gods did punish, and for impudence
They gaue this doome that was agreed by all,
The smell of the white Rose should be but small.
His haire was bushie, but it was not long,
The Nymphs had done his tresses mighty wrong:
For as it grew, they puld away his haire,
And made abilliments of gold to weare.
His eyes were Cupids: for vntill his birth,

Cupid had eyes, and liu'd vpon the earth,
Till on a day, when the great Queene of loue
Was by her white doues drawn from heauen aboue,
Vnto the top of the Idalian hill,
To see how well the Nymphs their charge fulfill,
And whether they had done the goddesse right,
In nursing of her sweet Hermaphrodite:
VVhom when she saw, although complete & full,
Yet she complaynd, his eyes were somewhat dull:
And therefore, more the wanton boy to grace,
She puld the sparkling eyes from Cupids face,
Fayning a cause to take away his sight,
Because the Ape would sometimes shoot for spight.
But Venus set those eyes in such a place,
As grac'd those cleare eyes with a clearer face.
For his white hand each goddesse did him woo:
For it was whiter then the driuen snow:
His legge was straighter then the thigh of loue:
And he farre fairer then the god of loue.
When first this wel-shapt boy, beauties chiefe king,
Had seene the labour of the fifteenth spring,
How curiously it paynted all the earth,
He 'gan to trauaile from his place of birth,
Leauing the stately hils where he was nurst,
And where the Nymphs had brought him vp at first:
He lou'd to trauaile to the coasts vnknowne,
To see the regions farre beyond his owne,
Seeking cleare watry springs to bathe him in:
(For he did loue to wash his iuory skinne)
The louely Nymphes haue oft times seene him swimme,
And closely stole his clothes from off the brim,
Because the wanton wenches would so fayne
See him come nak'd to ask his clothes againe.
He lou'd besides to see the Lycian grounds,
And know the wealthy Carians vtmost bounds.
Vsing to trauaile thus, one day he found
A cristall brook, that tril'd along the ground,
A brooke, that in reflection did surpasse
The cleare reflection of the clearest glasse.
About the side there grew no foggy reedes,
Nor was the fount compast with barren weedes:
But liuing turfe grew all along the side,
And grasse that euer flourisht in his pride.
Within this brook a beauteous Nymph did dwell,
Who for her comely feature did excell;
So faire she vvas, of such a pleasing grace,
So straight a body, and so sweet a face,
So soft a belly, such a lustie thigh,

So large a forehead, such a cristall eye,
So soft and moyst a hand, so smooth a brest,
So faire a cheeke, so well in all the rest,
That Iupiter would reuell in her bowre,
Were he to spend againe his golden showre:
Her teeth were whiter then the mornings milke,
Her lip was softer then the softest silke,
Her haire as farre surpast the burnisht gold,
As siluer doth excell the basest mold:
Ioue courted her for her translucent eye,
And told her, he would place her in the skye,
Promising her, if she would be his loue,
He would ingraue her in the heauen aboue,
Telling this louely Nymph, that if he would,
He could deceiue her in a showre of gold,
Or like a Swanne come to her naked bed,
And so deceiue her of her maiden-head:
But yet, because he thought that pleasure best,
Where each consenting ioynes each louing brest,
He would put off that all-commaunding crowne,
Whose terrour strooke th'aspiring Giants downe,
That glittereing crown, whose radiant sight did tosse
Great Pelion from the top of mighty Osse,
He would depose from his world-swaying head,
To taste the amorous pleasures of her bed:
This added he besides, the more to grace her,
Like a bright starre he would in heauens vault place her.
By this the proud lasciuious Nymph was mou'd,
Perceiuing by great Ioue shee was belou'd,
And hoping as a starre she should ere long,
Be sterne or gracious to the Sea-mans song,
(For mortals still are subiect to their eye,
And what it sees, they striue to get as hie
She was contented that almighty Ioue
Should haue the first and best fruits of her loue:
(For women may be likened to the yeere,
Whose first fruits still do make the dayntiest cheere)
But yet Astræa first should plight her troth,
For the performance of loues sacred oth.
(Iust times decline, and all good dayes are dead,
When heauenly othes had need be warranted)
This heard great Iupiter and lik'd it well,
And hastily he seeks Astræas cell,
About the massie earth searching her towre:
But she had long since left this earthly bowre,
And flew to heauen aboue, lothing to see
The sinfull actions of humanitie.
Which when Ioue did perceiue, he left the earth,

And flew vp to the place of his owne birth,
The burning heauenly throne, where he did spy
Astræas palace in the glittering skie.
This stately towre was builded vp on hie,
Farre from the reach of any mortall eye;
And from the palace side there did distill
A little water, through a little quill,
The dewe of iustice, which did seldome fall,
And when it dropt, the drops were very small.
Glad was great Ioue when he beheld her towre,
Meaning a while to rest him in her bowre;
And therefore sought to enter at her dore:
But there was such a busie rout before;
Some seruing men, and some promooters bee,
That he could passe no foote without a fee:
But as he goes, he reaches out his hands,
And payes each one in order as he stands;
And still, as he was paying those before,
Some slipt againe betwixt him and the dore.
At length (with much adoo) he past them all,
And entred straight into a spacious hall,
Full of dark angles, and of hidden wayes,
Crooked Maranders, infinite delays;
All which delayes and entries he must passe,
Ere he could come where iust Astræa was.
All these being past by his immortall wit,
Without her doore he sawe a porter sit,
An aged man, that long time there had beene,
Who vs'd to search all those that entred in,
And still to euery one he gaue this curse,
None must see Iustice but with emptie purse.
This man searcht Ioue for his owne priuate gaine,
To haue the money which did yet remaine,
Which was but small: for much was spent before
On the tumultuous rout that kept the dore.
When he had done, he broght him to the place
Where he should see diuine Astræas face.
Then the great King of gods and men in went,
And saw his daughter Venus there lament,
And crying lowd for iustice, whom Ioue found
Kneeling before Astræa on the ground,
And still she cry'd and beg'd for a iust doome
Against blacke Vulcan, that vnseemely groome,
Whome she had chosen for her onely loue,
Though she was daughter to great thundering Ioue:
And thought the fairest goddesse, yet content
To marrie him, though weake and impotent;
But for all this they alwayes were at strife:

For euermore he ralyd at her his wife,
Telling her still, Thou art no wife of mine,
Anothers strumpet, Mars his concubine.
By this Astræa spyde almighty Ioue,
And bow'd her finger to the Queene of loue,
To cease her sute, which she would hear anon,
When the great King of all the world was gone.
Then she descended from her stately throne,
Which seat was builded all of Iasper stone,
And o're the seat was paynted all aboue,
The wanton vnseene stealths of amorous Ioue;
There might a man behold the naked pride
Of louely Venus in the vales of Ide,
When Pallas, and Ioues beauteous wife and she
Stroue for the prise of beauties raritie:
And there lame Vulcan and his Cyclops stroue
To make the thunderbolts for mighty Ioue:
From this same stately throne she down descended,
And sayd, The griefs of Ioue should be amended,
Asking the King of gods what lucklesse cause,
What great contempt of states, what breach of lawes
(For sure she thought, some vncouth cause befell,
That made him visit poore Astræas cell)
Troubled his thought: and if she might decide it,
VVho vext great, Ioue, he deareley should abide it.
Ioue onely thankt her, and beganne to show
His cause of comming (for each one doth know
The longing words of Louers are not many,
If they desire to be inioyd of any.
Telling Astræa, It might now befall,
That she might make him blest, that blesseth all:
For as he walk'd vpon the flowry earth,
To which his owne hands whilome gaue a birth,
To see how streight he held it and how iust
He rold this massy pondrous heape of dust,
He laid him downe by a coole riuer side,
Whose pleasant water did so gently slide
With such soft whispering: for the brook was deepe,
That it had lul'd him in a heauenly sleepe.
When first he laid him downe, there was none neere him:
(for he did call before, but none could heare him)
But a faire Nymph was bathing when he wak'd,
(Here sigh'd great Ioue, and after brought forth) nak'd,
He seeing lou'd, the Nymph yet here did rest,
Where iust Astræa might make loue be blest,
If she would passe her faithfull word so farre,
As that great Ioue should make the mayd a starre.
Astræa yeelded: at which Ioue was pleas'd,

And all his longing hopes and feares were eas'd.
Ioue tooke his leaue, and parted from her sight,
Whose thoughts were ful of louers sweet delight,
And she ascended to her throne aboue,
To heare the griefes of the great Queene of loue.
But she was satisfide, and would no more
Rayle at her husband as she did before:
But forth she tript apace, because she stroue,
With her swift feet to ouertake great loue,
She skipt so nimbly as she went to looke him,
That at the palace doore she ouertooke him,
Which way was plaine and broade as they went out,
And now they could see no tumultuous rout.
Here Venus fearing, lest the loue of loue
Should make this mayd be plac'd in heauen aboue,
Because she thought this Nymph so wondrous bright,
That she would dazel her accustom'd light:
And fearing now she should not first be seene
Of all the glittering starres as shee had beene,
But that the wanton Nymph would eu'ry night
Be first that should salute eche mortal sight,
Began to tell great loue, she grieu'd to see
The heauen so full of his iniquity,
Complayning that eche strumpet now was grac'd,
And with immortall goddesses was plac'd,
Intreating him to place in heauen no more
Eche wanton strumpet and lasciuious whore.
Ioue mad with loue, harkned not what she sayd,
His thoughts were so intangled with the mayd,
But furiously he to his palace lept,
Being minded there till morning to haue slept:
For the next morne, as soone as Phoebus rayes
Should yet shine coole, by reason of the seas,
And ere the parting teares of Thætis bed,
Should be quite shak't from off his glittring head,
Astræa promis'd to attend great loue,
At his owne Palace in the heauen aboue,
And at that Palace she would set her hand
To what the loue-sick god should her command:
But to descend to earth she did deny,
She loath'd the sight of any mortall eye,
And for the compasse of the earthly round,
She would not set one foot vpon the ground.
Therefore loue meant to rise but with the sunne,
Yet thought it long vntill the night was done.
In the meane space Venus was drawne along
By her white Doues vnto the sweating throng
Of hammering Black-smithes, at the lofty hill

Of stately Etna, whose top burneth still:
(For at that burning mountaynes glittring top,
Her cripple husband Vulcan kept his shop)
To him she went, and so collogues that night
With the best straines of pleasures sweet delight,
That ere they parted, she made Vulcan sweare
By dreadfull Stix, an othe the gods do feare,
If Ioue would make the mortall mayd a starre,
Himselfe should frame his instruments of warre,
And tooke his othe by blacke Cocitus Lake,
He neuer more a thunder-bolt would make:
For Venus so this night his sences pleas'd,
That now he thought his former griefs were eas'd.
She with her hands the black-smiths body bound,
And with her Iu'ry armes she twyn'd him round,
And still the faire Queene with a prety grace,
Disperst her sweet breath o're his swarty face:
Her snowy armes so well she did display,
That Vulcan thought they melted as they lay.
Vntill the morne in this delight they lay:
Then vp they got, and hasted fast away
In the white Chariot of the Queene of loue,
Towards the Palace of great thundring Ioue,
Where they did see diuine Astræa stand,
To passe her word for what Ioue should command.
In limpt the Blacke-smith, after stept his Queene,
Whose light arrayment was of louely greene.
When they were in, Vulcan began to sweare
By othes that Iupiter himselfe doth feare,
If any whore in heauens bright vault were seene,
To dimme the shining of his beauteous Queene,
Each mortall man should the great gods disgrace,
And mocke almightie Ioue vnto his face,
And Giants should enforce bright heauen to fall,
Ere he would frame one thunderbolt at all.
Ioue did intreat him that he would forbeare.
The more he spoke, the more did Vulcan sweare.
Ioue heard his words, and 'gan to make his mone,
That mortall men would pluck him from his throne,
Or else he must incurre this plague, he said,
Quite to forgoe the pleasure of the mayd:
And once he thought, rather than lose her blisses,
Her heauenly sweets, her most delicious kisses,
Her soft embraces, and the amorous nights,
That he should often spend in her delights,
He would be quite thrown down by mortal hands,
From the blest place where his bright palace stands.
But afterwards hee saw with better sight,

He should be scorn'd by euery mortall wight,
If he should want his thunderbolts, to beate
Aspiring mortals from his glittering seate:
Therefore the god no more did woo or proue her,
But left to seeke her loue, though not to loue her.
Yet he forgot not that he woo'd the lasse,
But made her twise as beauteous as she was,
Because his wonted loue he needs would shew.
This haue I heard, but yet scarce thought it true.
And whether her cleare beautie was so bright,
That it could dazel the immortall sight
Of gods, and make them for her loue despaire,
I do not know; but sure the maid was faire.
Yet the faire Nymph was neuer seene resort
Vnto the sauage and the bloudy sport
Of chaste Diana, nor was euer wont
To bend a bow, nor euer did she hunt,
Nor did she euer striue with pretie cunning,
To ouergoe her fellow Nymphs in running:
For she was the faire water-Nymph alone,
That vnto chaste Diana was vnknowne.
It is reported, that her fellowes vs'd
To bid her (though the beauteous Nymph refus'd)
To take, or painted quiuers or a dart,
And put her lazy idlenesse apart.
Nor tooke she painted quiuers, nor a dart,
Nor put her lazy idlenesse apart,
But in her cristall fountaine oft she swimmes,
And oft she washes o're her snowy limmes:
Sometimes she com'b her soft discheuel'd hayre,
Which with a fillet tide she oft did weare:
But sometimes loose she did it hang behind,
When she was pleas'd to grace the Easterne wind:
For vp and downe it would her tresses hurle,
And as she went, it made her loose hayre curl:
Oft in the water did she looke her face,
And oft she vs'd to practise what quaint grace
Might well become her, and what comely feature
Might be best fitting so diuine a creature.
Her skinne was with a thinne vaile ouerthrowne,
Through which her naked beauty clearly shone.
She vs'd in this light rayment as she was,
To spread her body on the dewy grasse:
Sometimes by her owne fountaine as she walkes,
She nips the flowres from off the fertile stalkes,
And with a garland of the sweating vine,
Sometimes she doth her beauteous front in-twine:
But she was gathering flowres with her white hand,

When she beheld Hermaphroditus stand
By her cleare fountaine, wondring at the sight,
That there was any brooke could be so bright:
For this was the bright riuer where the boy
Did dye himselfe, that he could not enioy
Himselfe in pleasure, nor could taste the blisses
Of his owne melting and delicious kisses.
Here she did see him, and by Venus law,
She did desire to haue him as she saw:
But the fayre Nymph had neuer seene the place,
Where the boy was, nor his inchanting face,
But by an vncouth accident of loue
Betwixt great Phoebus and the sonne of Ioue,
Light -headed Bacchus: for vpon a day,
As the boy-god was keeping on his way,
Bearing his Vine leaues and his Iuie bands,
To Naxos, where his house and temple stands,
He saw the Nymph, and seeing, he did stay,
And threw his leaues and Iuie bands away,
Thinking at first she was of heauenly birth,
Some goddesse that did liue vpon the earth,
Virgin Diana that so liuely shone,
When she did court her sweet Endimion:
But he a god, at last did plainely see,
She had no marke of immortalitie.
Vnto the Nymph went the yong god of wine,
Whose head was chaf'd so with the bleeding vine,
That now, or feare or terrour had he none,
But 'gan to court her as she sate alone:
Fayrer then fayrest (thus began his speech)
Would but your radiant eye please to inrich
My eye with looking, or one glaunce to giue,
Whereby my other parts might feede and liue,
Or with one sight my sences to inspire,
Far liuelier then the stole Promethean fire;
Then I might liue, then by the sunny light
That should proceed from thy thrise-radiant sight,
I might suruiue to ages; but that missing,
(At that same word he would haue faine bin kissing)
I pine, fayre Nymph: O neuer let me dye
For one poore glaunce from thy translucent eye,
Farre more transparent then the clearest brooke.
The Nymph was taken with his golden hooke:
Yet she turn'd backe, and would haue tript away;
But Bacchus forc't the louely mayd to stay,
Asking her why she struggled to be gone,
Why such a Nymph should wish to be alone?
Heauen neuer made her faire, that she should vaunt

She kept all beautie, it would neuer graunt
She should be borne so beauteous from her mother,
But to reflect her beauty on another:
Then with a sweet kisse cast thy beames on mee,
And Ile reflect then backe againe on thee.
At Naxos stands my Temple and my Shrine,
Where I do presse the lusty swelling Vine,
There with green Iuie shall thy head be bound,
And with the red Grape be incircled round;
There shall Silenus sing vnto thy praise,
His drunken reeling songs and tickling layes.
Come hither, gentle Nymph. Here blusht the maid,
And faine she would haue gone, but yet she staid.
Bacchus perceiued he had o'ercome the lasse,
And downe he throwes her in the dewy grasse,
And kist the helplesse Nymph vpon the ground,
And would haue stray'd beyond that lawful bound.
This saw bright Phœbus: for his glittering eye
Sees all that lies below the starry skye;
And for an old affection that he bore
Vnto this louely Nymph long time before,
(For he would ofttimes in his circle stand,
To sport himselfe vpon her snowy hand)
He kept her from the sweets of Bacchus bed,
And 'gainst her will he sau'd her maiden-head.
Bacchus perceiuing this apace did hie
Vnto the Palace of swift Mercury:
But he did find him farre below his birth,
Drinking with theiues and catch-poles on the earth;
And they were drinking what they stole to day,
In consultation for to morrowes prey.
To him went youthful Bacchus, and begun
To shew his cause of griefe against the Sunne,
How he bereft him of his heauenly blisses,
His sweet delights, his Nectar-flowing kisses,
And other sweeter sweetes that he had wonne,
But for the malice of the bright-fac't Sunne,
Intreating Mercury by all the loue,
That had bene borne amongst the sonnes of Ioue,
Of which they two were part, to stand his friend,
Against the god that did him so offend:
The quaint-tongu'd issue of great Atlas race,
Swift Mercury, that with delightfull grace,
And pleasing accents of his fayned tongue,
Hath oft reform'd a rude vnciuill throng
Of mortals; that great messenger of Ioue,
And all the meaner gods that dwell aboue:
He whose acute wit was so quicke and sharpe

In the inuention of the crooked Harpe:
He that's so cunning with his iesting slights,
To steale from heauenly gods or earthly wights,
Bearing a great hate in his grieued brest,
Against that great commaunder of the West,
Bright-fac't Apollo: for vpon a day,
Yong Mercury did steale his beasts away:
Which the great god perceiuing, streight did shew
The pearcing arrowes and the fearefull bow
That kild great Pithon, & with that did threat him,
To bring his beast againe, or he would beat him.
Which Mercury perceiuing, vnespide,
Did closely steale his arrowes from his side.
For this olde grudge, he was the easlyer wonne
To helpe young Bacchus 'gainst the fierie Sunne.
And now the Sunne was in the middle way,
And had o'ercome the one halfe of the day,
Scorching so hot vpon the reeking sand,
That lies vpon the neere Egyptian land,
That the hot people burnt e'ne from their birth,
Do creepe againe into their mother earth,
When Mercury did take his powerfull wand,
His charming Cadusæus in his hand,
And a thick Beuer which he vs'd to weare,
When ought from loue he to the Sunne did beare,
That did protect him from the piercing light,
Which did proceed from Phoebus glittering sight.
Clad in these powerfull ornaments he flies,
With out-stretcht wings vp to the azure skies:
Where seeing Phoebus in his orient shrine,
He did so well reuenge the god of wine,
That whil'st the Sun wonders his Chariot reeles,
The craftie god had stole away his wheeles.
Which when he did perceiue, he downe did slide,
(Laying his glittering Coronet aside)
From the bright spangled firmament aboue,
To seeke the Nymph that Bacchus so did loue,
And found her looking in her watry glasse,
To see how cleare her radiant beauty was:
And, for he had but little time to stay,
Because he meant to finish out his day,
At the first sight he 'gan to make his mone,
Telling her how his fiery wheeles were gone;
Promising her, if she would but obtaine
The wheeles, that Mercury had stolne, againe,
That he might end his day, she should enioy
The heauenly sight of the most beauteous boy
That euer was. The Nymph was pleas'd with this,

Hoping to reape some vnaccustom'd blisse
By the sweet pleasure that she should enioy,
In the blest sight of such a melting boy.
Therefore at his request she did obtaine
The burning wheeles, that he had lost, againe:
VVhich when he had receiu'd, he left the land,
And brought them thither where his Coach did stand,
And there he set them on: for all this space,
The horses had not stirr'd from out their place.
VVhich when he saw, he wept and 'gan to say,
VVould Mercury had stole my wheeles away,
When Phaeton my hare-brain'd issue tride,
What a laborious thing it vvas to guide
My burning chariot, then he might haue pleas'd me,
And of one fathers griefe he might haue eas'd me:
For then the Steeds would haue obayd his will,
Or else at least they would haue rested still.
When he had done, he tooke his whip of steele,
Whose bitter smart he made his horses feele:
For he did lash so hard, to end the day,
That he was quickly at the Westerne sea,
And there with Thætis did he rest a space,
For he did neuer rest in any place
Before that time: but euer since his wheeles
Were stole away, his burning chariot reeles
Tow'rds the declining of the parting day:
Therefore he lights and mends them in the sea.
And though the poets fayne, that loue did make
A treble night for faire Alcmena's sake,
That he might sleepe securely with his loue;
Yet sure the long night was vnknowne to loue:
But the Sunnes wheeles one day disordred more,
Were thrise as long amending as before.
Now was the Sunne inuiron'd with the Sea,
Cooling his watrie tresses as he lay,
And in dread Neptunes kingdome while he sleeps,
Faire Thætis clips him in the watry deeps,
The Mayre-maids and the Tritons of the West,
Strayning their voyces, to make Titan rest.
And while the blacke night with her pitchie hand,
Tooke iust possession of the swarfie land:
He spent the darkesome howres in this delight,
Giuing his power vp to the gladsome night:
For ne're before he was so truely blest,
To take an houre or one poore minutes rest.
But now the burning god this pleasure feeles,
By reason of his newly crazed wheeles,
There must he stay vntill lame Vulcan send

The fierie wheeles which he had tooke to mend.
Now al the night the Smith so hard had wrought,
That ere the Sunne could wake, his wheeles were brought.
Titan being pleas'd with rest, and not to rise,
And loth to open yet his slumbring eyes:
And yet perceiuing how the longing sight
Of mortals wayted for his glittring light,
He sent Aurora from him to the skie,
To giue a glimsing to each mortall eye.
Aurora much asham'd of that same place
That great Apollos light was wont to grace,
Finding no place to hide her shamefull head,
Paynted her chaste cheeks with a blushing red,
Which euer since remain'd vpon her face,
In token of her new receiu'd disgrace:
Therefore she not so white as she had beene,
Lothing of eu'ry mortall to be seene,
No sooner can the rosie fingred morne
Kisse eu'ry flowre that by her dew is borne,
But from her golden window she doth peepe,
When the most part of earthly creatures sleepe.
By this, bright Titan opened had his eyes,
And 'gan to ierke his horses through the skies,
And taking in his hand his fierie whip,
He made AEous and swift AEthon skip
So fast, that straight he dazled had the sight
Of faire Aurora, glad to see his light.
And now the Sunne in all his fierie haste,
Did call to mind his promise lately past,
And all the vowes and othes that he did passe
Vnto faire Salmacis, the beauteous lasse:
For he had promis'd her she should enioy
So louely faire, and such a well shapt boy,
As ne're before his owne all-seeing eye
Saw from his bright seate in the starry skye:
Remembring this, he sent the boy that way,
Where the cleare fountain of the fayre Nymph lay.
There was he come to seeke some pleasing brooke.
No sooner came he, but the Nymph was strooke:
And though she hasted to imbrace the boy,
Yet did the Nymph awhile deferre her ioy,
Till she had bound vp her loose flagging haire,
And ordred well the garments she did weare,
Fayning her count'nance with a louers care,
And did deserue to be accounted fayre.
And thus much spake she while the boy abode:
O boy, most worthy to be thought a god,
Thou mayst inhabit in the glorious place

Of gods, or maist proceed from human race:
Thou mayst be Cupid, or the god of wine,
That lately woo'd me with the swelling vine:
But whosoe're thou art, O happy he,
That was so blest, to be a sire to thee;
Thy happy mother is most blest of many,
Blessed thy sisters, if her wombe bare any,
Both fortunate, and O thrise happy shee,
Whose too much blessed breasts gaue suck to thee:
If any wife with thy sweet bed be blest,
O, she is farre more happy then the rest;
If thou hast any, let my sport be sto'ne,
Or else let me be she, if thou haue none.
Here did she pause a while, and then she sayd,
Be not obdurate to a silly mayd.
A flinty heart within a smowy brest,
Is like base mold lockt in a golden chest:
They say the eye's the Index of the heart,
And shewes th'affection of each inward part:
There loue playes liuely, there the little god
Hath a cleare cristall Palace of abode.
O barre him not from playing in thy heart,
That sports himselfe vpon eche outward part.
Thus much she spake, & then her tongue was husht.
At her loose speach Hermaphroditus blusht:
He knew not what loue was, yet loue did shame him,
Making him blush, and yet his blush became him:
Then might a man his shamefast colour see,
Like the ripe apple on the sunny tree,
Or Iuory dide o're with a pleasing red,
Or like the pale Moone being shadowed.
By this, the Nymph recouer'd had her tongue,
That to her thinking lay in silence long,
And sayd, Thy cheeke is milde, O be thou so,
Thy cheeke, saith I, then do not answere no,
Thy cheeke doth shame, then doe thou shame, she sayd,
It is a mans shame to deny a mayd.
Thou look'st to sport with Venus in her towre,
And be belou'd of euery heauenly powre.
Men are but mortals, so are women too,
Why should your thoughts aspire more than ours doo?
For sure they doe aspire: Else could a youth,
Whose count'nance is so full of spotlesse truth,
Be so relentlesse to a virgins tongue?
Let me be woo'd by thee but halfe so long,
With halfe those tearmes doe but my loue require,
And I will easly graunt thee thy desire.
Ages are bad, when men become so slow,

That poore vnskillful mayds are forc't to woo.
Her radiant beauty and her subtill arte
S deepely strooke Hermaphroditus heart,
That she had wonne his loue, but that the light
Of her translucent eyes did shine too bright:
For long he look'd vpon the louely mayd,
And at the last Hermaphroditus sayd,
How should I loue thee, when I doe espie
A farre more beauteous Nymph hid in thy eye?
When thou doost loue, let not that Nymph be nie thee;
Nor when thou woo'st, let not that Nymph be by thee:
Or quite obscure her from thy louers face,
Or hide her beauty in a darker place.
By this, the Nymph perceiu'd he did espie
None but himselfe reflected in her eye,
And, for himselfe no more she meant to shew him,
She shut her eyes & blind-fold thus did woo him:
Fayre boy, thinke not thy beauty can dispence
With any payne due to a bad offence;
Remember how the gods punisht that boy
That scorn'd to let a beauteous Nymph enioy
Her long wisht pleasure, for the peeuish elfe,
Lou'd of all other, needs would loue himselfe.
So mayst thou loue, perhaps thou mayst be blest;
By graunting to a lucklesse Nymphs request:
Then rest awhile with me amid these weeds.
The Sunne that sees all, sees not louers deeds;
Phoebus is blind when loue-sports are begun,
And neuer sees vntill their sports be done:
Beleeue me, boy, thy blood is very stayd,
That art so loth to kisse a youthfull mayd.
Wert thou a mayd, and I a man, Ile show thee,
With what a manly boldnesse I could woo thee,
Fayrer then loues Queene, thus I would begin,
Might not my ouer-boldnesse be a sinne,
I would intreat this fauor, if I could,
Thy rosiat cheeke a little to behold:
Then would I beg a touch, and then a kisse,
And then a lower, yet a higher blisse:
Then would I aske what loue and Læda did,
When like a Swan the craftie god was hid?
What came he for? why did he there abide?
Surely I thinke hee did not come to chide:
He came to see her face, to talke, and chat,
To touch, to kisse: came he for nought but that?
Yea, something else: what was it he would haue?
That which all men of maydens ought to craue.
This sayd, her eye-lids wide she did display:

But in this space the boy was runne away:
The wanton speeches of the louely lasse
Forc't him for shame to hide him in the grasse.
When she perceiu'd she could not see him neere her,
When she had cal'd and yet he could not heare her,
Look how when Autumne comes, a little space
Paleth the red blush of the Summers face,
Tearing the leaues the Summers couering,
Three months in weauing by the curious spring,
Making the grasse his greene locks go to wracke,
Tearing each ornament from off his backe;
So did she spoyle the garments she did weare,
Tearing whole ounces of her golden hayre:
She thus deluded of her longed blisse,
With much adoo at last she vttred this:
Why wert thou bashfull, boy? Thou hast no part
Shewes thee to be of such a female heart.
His eye is gray, so is the mornings eye,
That blusheth alwayes when the day is nye.
Then his gray eye's the cause: that cannot be:
The gray-ey'd morne is farre more bold then he:
For with a gentle dew from heauens bright towre,
It gets the mayden-head of eu'ry flowre.
I would to God, he were the rosiat morne,
And I a flowre from out the earth new-borne?
His face was smooth; Narcissus face was so,
And he was carelesse of a sad Nymphs woe.
Then that's the cause; and yet that cannot be:
Youthfull Narcissus was more bold then he,
Because he dide for loue, though of his shade:
This boy nor loues himselfe, nor yet a mayd.
Besides, his glorious eye is wondrous bright;
So is the fierie and all-seeing light
Of Phœbus, who at eu'ry mornings birth
Blusheth for shame vpon the sullen earth.
Then that's the cause; and yet that cannot be:
The fierie Sunne is farre more bold then he;
He nightly kisseth Thætis in the sea:
All know the story of Leucothoe.
His cheeke is red: so is the fragrant Rose,
Whose ruddie cheeke with ouer-blushing gloes:
Then that's the cause; and yet that cannot bee:
Eche blushing Rose is farre more bold then he,
Whose boldnesse may be plainely seene in this,
The ruddy Rose is not asham'd to kisse;
For alwayes when the day is new begun,
The spreading Rose will kisse the morning Sun.
This sayd, hid in the grasse she did espie him,

And stumbling with her will, she fel down by him,
And with her wanton talke, because he woo'd not,
Beg'd that, which he poore nouice vnderstood not:
And, for she could not get a greater blisse,
She did intreate a least a sisters kisse;
But still the more she did the boy beseech,
The more he powted at her wanton speech.
At last the Nymph began to touch his skin,
Whiter then mountaine snow hath euer bin,
And did in purenesse that cleare spring surpasse,
Wherein Acteon saw th'Arcadian lasse.
Thus did she dally long, till at the last,
In her moyst palme she lockt his white hand fast:
Then in her hand his wrest she 'gan to close,
When through his pulses strait the warm bloud gloes,
Whose youthfull musike fanning Cupids fire,
In her warme brest kindled a fresh desire.
Then did she lift her hand vnto his brest,
A part as white and youthfull as the rest,
Where, as his flowry breath still comes and goes,
She felt his gentle heart pant through his clothes.
At last she tooke her hand from off that part,
And sayd, It panted like anothers heart.
Why should it be more feeble, and lesse bold?
Why should the bloud about it be more cold?
Nay sure, that yeelds, onely thy tongue denyes,
And the true fancy of thy heart belyes.
Then did she lift her hand vnto his chin,
And prays'd the prety dimpling of his skin:
But straight his chin she 'gan to ouerslip,
When she beheld the rednesse of his lip;
And sayd, thy lips are soft, presse them to mine,
And thou shalt see they are as soft as thine.
Then would she faine haue gone vnto his eye,
But still his ruddy lip standing so nie,
Drew her hand backe, therefore his eye she mist,
'Ginning to claspe his neck, and would haue kist;
But then the boy did struggle to be gone,
Vowing to leaue her and that place alone.
But then bright Salmacis began to feare,
And sayd, Fayre stranger, I wil leaue thee here
Amid these pleasant places all alone.
So turning back, she fayned to be gone;
But from his sight she had no power to passe,
Therefore she turn'd and hid her in the grasse,
When to the ground bending her snow-white knee,
The glad earth gaue new coates to euery tree.
He then supposing he was all alone,

(Like a young boy that is espy'd of none)
Runnes here, and there, then on the bankes doth looke,
Then on the cristall current of the brooke,
Then with his foote he toucht the siluer streames,
Whose drowsy waues made musike in their dreames,
And, for he was not wholy in, did weepe,
Talking alowd and babbling in their sleepe:
Whose pleasant coolnesse when the boy did feele,
He thrust his foote downe lower to the heele:
O'ercome with whose sweet noyse, he did begin
To strip his soft clothes from his tender skin,
When strait the scorching Sun wept teares of brine,
Because he durst not touch him with his shine,
For feare of spoyling that same Iu'ry skin,
Whose whitenesse he so much delighted in;
And then the Moone, mother of mortall ease,
Would fayne haue come from the Antipodes,
To haue beheld him naked as he stood,
Ready to leape into the siluer flood;
But might not: for the lawes of heauen deny,
To shew mens secrets to a womans eye:
And therefore was her sad and gloomy light
Confin'd vnto the secret-keeping night.
When beauteous Salmacis awhile had gaz'd
Vpon his naked corps, she stood amaz'd,
And both her sparkling eyes burnt in her face,
Like the bright Sunne reflected in a glasse:
Scarce can she stay from running to the boy,
Scarce can she now deferre her hoped ioy;
So fast her youthfull bloud playes in her vaynes,
That almost mad, she scarce herselfe contaynes.
When young Hermaphroditus as he stands,
Clapping his white side with his hollow hands,
Leapt liuely from the land, whereon he stood,
Into the mayne part of the cristall flood.
Like Iu'ry then his snowy body was,
Or a white Lilly in a christall glasse.
Then rose the water Nymph from where she lay,
As hauing wonne the glory of the day,
And her light garments cast from off her skin,
Hee's mine, she cry'd, and so leapt spritely in.
The flattering Iuy who did euer see
Inclaspe the huge trunke of an aged tree,
Let him behold the young boy as he stands,
Inclaspt in wanton Salmacis's hands,
Betwixt those Iu'ry armes she lockt him fast,
Striuing to get away, till at the last,
Fondling, she sayd, why striu'st thou to be gone?

Why shouldst thou so desire to be alone?
Thy cheeke is neuer fayre, when none is by:
For what is red and white, but to the eye:
And for that cause the heauens are darker at night,
Because all creatures close their weary sight;
For there's no mortall can so earely rise,
But still the morning waytes vpon his eyes.
The earely-rising and soone-singing Larke
Can neuer chaunt her sweete notes in the darke,
For sleepe she ne're so little or so long,
Yet still the morning will attend her song.
All creatures that beneath bright Cinthia be,
Haue appetite vnto society;
The ouerflowing waues would haue a bound
Within the confines of the spacious ground,
And all their shady currents would be plaste
In hollow of the solitary vaste,
But what they lothe to let their soft streames sing,
Where non can heare their gentle murmuring.
Yet still the boy regardlesse what she sayd,
Struggled apace to ouerswimme the mayd.
Which when the Nymph perceiu'd she 'gan to say,
Struggle thou mayst, but neuer get away.
So graunt, iust gods, that neuer day may see
The separation twixt this boy and mee.
The gods did heare her pray'r and feele her woe;
And in one body they began to grow.
She felt his youthfull bloud in euery vaine;
And he felt hers warme his colde brest againe.
And euer since was womans loue so blest,
That it will draw bloud from the strongerst brest.
Nor man nor mayd now could they be esteem'd:
Neither, and either, might they well be deem'd,
When the young boy Hermaphroditus sayd,
VVith the set voyce of neither man nor mayd,
Swift Mercury, the author of my life,
And thou my mother Vulcans louely wife,
Let your poore offsprings latest breath be blest,
In but obtayning this his last request,
Grant that whoe're heated by Phoebus beames,
Shall come to coole him in these siluer streames,
May neuermore a manly shape retaine,
But halfe a virgine may returne againe.
His parents hark'ned to his last request,
And with that great power they the fountaine blest.
And since that time who in that fountaine swimmes,
A mayden smoothnesse seyzeth half his limmes.

A Sonnet

Flattering Hope, away and leave me,
She'll not come, thou dost deceive me;
Hark the cock crows, th' envious light
Chides away the silent night;
Yet she comes not, oh! how I tire
Betwixt cold fear and hot desire.

Here alone enforced to tarry
While the tedious minutes marry,
And get hours, those days and years,
Which I count with sighs and fears
Yet she comes not, oh! how I tire
Betwixt cold fear and hot desire.

Restless thoughts a while remove
Unto the bosom of my love,
Let her languish in my pain,
Fear and hope, and fear again;
Then let her tell me, in love's fire,
What torment's like unto desire?

Endless wishing, tedious longing,
Hopes and fears together thronging;
Rich in dreams, yet poor in waking,
Let her be in such a taking:
Then let her tell me in love's fire,
What torment's like unto desire?

Come then, Love, prevent day's eyeing,
My desire would fain be dying:
Smother me with breathless kisses,
Let me dream no more of blisses;
But tell me, which is in Love's fire
Best, to enjoy, or to desire?

The Glance

Cold Virtue guard me, or I shall endure
From the next glance a double calenture
Of fire and lust! Two flames, two Semeles,
Dwell in those eyes, whose looser glowing rays
Would thaw the frozen Russian into lust,

And parch tile negro's hotter blood to dust.
Dart not your bllls of wild-fire here; go throw
Those flakes upon the eunuch's colder snow,
Till he in active blood do boil as high
As he that made him so in jealousy.
When that loose queen of love did dress her eyes
In the most taking flame to the prize
At Ida; that faint glare to this desire
Burnt like a taper to the zone of fire:
And could she then the lustful youth have crowned
With thee his Helen, Troy had never found
Her fate in Sinon's fire; thy hotter eyes
Had made it burn a quicker sacrifice
To lust, whilst every glance in subtle wiles
Had shot itself like lightning through the piles.
Go blow upon some equal blood, and let
Earth's hotter ray engender and beget
New flames to dress the aged Paphians' quire,
And lend the world new Cupids borne on fire.
Dart no more here, those flatmes, nor strive to throw
Your fire on him who is immured in snow!
Those glances work on me like the weak shine
The frosty sun throws on the Appenine,
When the hill's active coldness doth go near
To freeze the glimmering taper to his sphere:
Each ray is lost on me, like the faint light
The glow-worm shoots at the cold breast of night.
Thus virtue can secure; but for that name
I had been now sin's martyr, and your flame.

The Indifferent

Never more will I protest,
To love a woman but in jest:
For as they cannot be true,
So, to give each man his due,
When the wooing fit is past
Their affection cannot last.

Therefore, if I chance to meet
With a mistress fair and sweet,
She my service shall obtain,
Loving her for love again:
Thus much liberty I crave,
Not to be a constant slave.

But when we have tried each other,
If she better like another,
Let her quickly change for me,
Then to change am I as free.
He or she that loves too long
Sell their freedom for a song.

On the Marriage of a Beauteous Young Gentlewoman with an Ancient Man

Fondly, too curious Nature, to adorn
Aurora with the blushes of the morn:
Why do her rosy lips breath gums and spice;
Unto the East, and sweet to Paradise?
Why do her eyes open the day? her hand
And voice intrance the panther, and command
Incensed winds; her breasts, the tents of love,
Smooth as the godded swan, or Venus' dove;
Soft as the balmy dew whose every touch
Is pregnant; but why those rich spoils, when such
Wonder and perfection must be led
A bridal captive unto Tithon's bed?
Ag'd, and deformed Tithon! must thy twine
Circle and blast at once what care and time
Had made for wonder? must pure beauty have
No other foil but ruin and a grave?
So have I seen the pride of Nature's store,
The orient pearl chained to the sooty Moor;
So hath the diamond's bright ray been set
In night, and wedded to the negro jet.
See, see, how thick those showers of pearl do fall
To weep her ransom, or her funeral,
Whose every treasured drop, congealed, might bring,
Freedom and ransom to a fettered kin,
While tyrant Wealth stands by, and laughs to see
How he can wed love and antipathy.
Hymen, thy pine burns with adulterate fire;
Thou and thy quivered boy did once conspire
To mingle equal flames, and then no shine
Of gold, but beauty, dressed the Paphian shrine;
Roses and lilies kiss'd; the amorous vine
Did with the fair and straight-limb'd elm entwine.

On the Tombs in Westminster Abbey

Mortality, behold and fear!

What a change of flesh is here!
Think how many royal bones
Sleep within this heap of stones:
Here they lie had realms and lands,
Who now want strength to stir their hands:
Where from their pulpits seal'd with dust
They preach, 'In greatness is no trust.'
Here 's an acre sown indeed
With the richest, royall'st seed
That the earth did e'er suck in
Since the first man died for sin:
Here the bones of birth have cried—
'Though gods they were, as men they died.'
Here are sands, ignoble things,
Dropt from the ruin'd sides of kings;
Here 's a world of pomp and state,
Buried in dust, once dead by fate.

To the True Patroness of All Poetry, Calliope

It is a statute in deep wisdom's lore,
That for his lines none should a patron chuse
By wealth and poverty, by less or more,
But who the same is able to peruse:
Nor ought a man his labour dedicate,
Without a true and sensible desert,
To any power of such a mighty state
But such a wise defendress as thou art
Thou great and powerful Muse, then pardon me
That I presume thy maiden cheek to stain
In dedicating such a work to thee,
Sprung from the issue of an idle brain:
I use thee as a woman ought to be,
I consecrate my idle hours to thee.

True Beauty

May I find a woman fair,
And her mind as clear as air,
If her beauty go alone,
'Tis to me as if't were none.

May I find a woman rich,
And not of too high a pitch;

If that pride should cause disdain,
Tell me, lover, where's thy gain?

May I find a woman wise,
And her falsehood not disguise;
Hath she wit as she hath will,
Double arm'd she is to ill.

May I find a woman kind,
And not wavering like the wind:
How should I call that love mine,
When 'tis his, and his, and thine?

May I find a woman true,
There is Bettutv's fairest hue,
There is Beauty, Love, and Wit:
Happy he can compass it.

Mr. Francis Beaumont's Letter to Ben Jonson

The sun, which doth the greatest comfort bring
To absent friends (because the self-same thing
They know they see, however absent), is
Here our best hay-maker (forgive me this,
It is our country style); in this warm shine
I lie, and dream of your full Mermaid wine.
Oh, we have water mixed with claret-lees,
Drink apt to bring in drier heresies
Than beer, good only for the sonnet strain,
With fustian metaphors to stuff the brain;
So mixed that given to the thirstiest one
'Twill not prove alms unless he have the stone.
I think with one draught man's invention fades,
Two cups had quite marred Homer's Iliads;
'Tis liquor that will find out Sutcliffe's wit,
Lie where it will, and make him write worse yet.
Filled with such moisture, in a grievous qualm,
Did Robert Wisdom write his singing psalm;
And so must I do this, and yet I think
It is a potion sent us down to drink
By special providence, keeps us from fights,
Makes us not laugh when we make legs to knights;
'Tis this that keeps our minds fit for our states,
A med'cine to obey our magistrates.
For we do live more free than you; no hate,
No envy of another's happy state

Moves us, we are all equal, every whit;
Of land, that God gives men here, is their wit,
If we consider fully, for our best
And gravest man will, with his main house-jest,
Scarce please you; we want subtlety to do
The city tricks—lie, hate, and flatter too.
Here are none that can bear a painted show,
Strike when you wink, and then lament the blow,
Who, like mills set the right way to grind,
Can make their gains alike with every wind.
Only some fellow with the subtlest pate
Amongst us, may perchance equivocate

At selling of a horse, and that's the most.
Methinks the little wit I had is lost
Since I saw you; for wit is like a rest
Held up at tennis, which men do the best
With the best gamesters. What things have we seen
Done at the Mermaid! heard words that have been
So nimble and so full of subtle flame,
As if that everyone from whence they came
Had meant to put his whole wit in a jest,
And had resolved to live a fool the rest
Of his dull life; then when there has been thrown
Wit able enough to justify the town
For three days past; wit that might warrant be
For the whole city to talk foolishly
Till that were cancelled, and when we were gone,
We left an air behind, which was alone
Able to make the two next companies
Right witty, though they were downright cockneys.
When I remember this, and see that now
The country gentlemen begin to allow
My wit for dry-bobs, then I needs must cry,
I see my days of ballading are nigh;
I can already riddle, and can sing
Catches, sell bargains, and I fear shall bring
Myself to speak the hardest words I find
Over as fast as any, with one wind
That takes no medicines. But one thought of thee
Makes me remember all these things to be
The wit of our young men, fellows that show
No part of good, yet utter all they know;
Who like trees and the guard have growing souls
Only; strong destiny, which all controls,
I hope hath left a better fate in store
For me, thy friend, than to live evermore
Banished unto this home; 'twill once again

Bring me to thee, who wilt make smooth and plain
The way of knowledge for me, and then I
Who have no good in me but simplicity,
Know that it will my greatest comfort be
To acknowledge all the rest to come from thee.

In Laudem Authoris

Like to the weake estate of a poore friend,
To whom sweet fortune hath bene euer slow,
Which dayly doth that happy howre attend,
When his poore state may his affection shew:
So fares my loue, not able as the rest,
To chaunt thy prayses in a lofty vayne,
Yet my poore Muse doth vow to doe her best,
And wanting wings, shee'le tread an humble strayne.
I thought at first her homely steps to rayse,
And for some blazing Epithites to looke,
But then I fear'd, that by such wondrous prayse,
Some men would grow suspicious of thy booke:
For hee that doth thy due deserts reherse,
Depriues that glory from thy worthy verse.

Lay A Garland On My Hearse

Lay a garland on my hearse,
Of the dismal yew,
Maidens, willow branches bear,
Say I died true.
My love was false, but I was firm
From my hour of birth;
Upon my buried body lie
Lightly, gentle earth.

The Conclusion

Sleep not too much; nor longer than asleep
Within thy bed thy lazy body keep;
For when thou, warm awake, shall feel it soft,
Fond cogitations will assail thee oft:
Then start up early, study, work, or write,
Let labour, others' toil, be thy delight.

Eat not to much, or if thou much dost eat,
Let it not be dainty or stirring meat;
Abstain from wine, although thou think it good,
It sets thy meat on fire, and stirs thy blood;
Use thyself much to bathe thy wanton limbs,
In coolest streams which o'er the gravel swims:
Be still in gravest company, and fly
The wanton rabble of the younger fry,
Whose lustful tricks will lead thee to delight
To think on love, where thou shalt perish quite;
Come not at all where many women are,
But, like a bird that lately 'scaped the snare,
Avoid their garish beauty fly with speed,
And learn by her that lately made thee bleed;
Be not too much alone, but if alone,
Get thee some modest book to look upon;
But do not read the lines of wanton men,
Poetry sets thy mind on fire again:
Abstain from songs and verses, and take heed
That not a line of love thou ever read.

An Elegy On the Death of the Virtuous Lady Elizabeth, Countess of Rutland

I may forget to drink, to eat, to sleep,
Remembering thee: but when I do, to weep
In well-weighed lines, that men shall at thy hearse
Envy the sorrow which brought forth my verse;
May my dull understanding have the might
Only to know her last was yesternight!
Rutland, the fair, is dead! and if to hear
The name of Sidney will more force a tear,
'Tis she that is so dead! and yet there be
Some more alive profess not poetry;
The statesmen and the lawyers of our time
Have business still, yet do it not in rhyme.
Can she be dead, and can there be of those
That are so dull to say their prayers in prose?
It is three days since she did feel Death's hand;
And yet this isle not feel the poet's land?
Hath this no new ones made? and are the old
At such a needful time as this grown cold?
They all say they would fain; but yet they plead
They cannot write, because their muse is dead.
Hear me then speak, which will take no excuse;
Sorrow can make a verse without a muse.
Why didst thou die so soon? O, pardon me,

I know it was the longest life to thee,
That e'er with modesty was called a span,
Since the Almighty left to strive with man;
Mankind is sent to sorrow; and thou hast
More of the business which thou cam'st for past,
Than all those aged women, which, yet quick,
Have quite outlived their own arithmetic.
As soon as thou couldst apprehend a grief,
There were enough to meet thee; and the chief
Blessing of women, marriage, was to thee
Nought but a sacrament of misery;
For whom thou hadst, if we may trust to fame,
Could nothing change about thee but thy name:
A name which who (that were again to do't)
Would change without a thousand joys to boot?
In all things else thou rather led'st a life
Like a betrothed virgin than a wife.
But yet I would have called thy fortune kind,
If it had only tried the settled mind
With present crosses: not the loathed thought
Of worse to come, or past, then might have wrough
Thy best remembrance to have cast an eye
Back with delight upon thine infancy.
But thou hadst, ere thou knew'st the use of tears,
Sorrow laid up against thou cam'st to years;
Ere thou wert able who thou wert to tell,
By a sad war thy noble father fell,
In a dull clime, which did not understand
What 'twas to venture him to save a land.
He left two children, who for virtue, wit,
Beauty, were loved of all; thee and his wit:
Two was too few; yet death hath from us took
Thee, a more faultless issue than his book,
Which now the only living thing we have
From him, we'll see, shall never find a grave
As thou hast done. Alas! 'would it might be
That books their sexes had, as well as we,
That we might see this married to the worth,
And many poems like itself bring forth!
But this vain wish divinity controuls;
For neither to the angels, nor to souls,
Nor anything he meant should ever live,
Did the wise God of nature sexes give.
Then with his everlasting work alone
We must content ourselves, since she is gone;
Gone, like the day thou diedst upon; and we
May call that back again as soon as thee.
Who should have looked to this? Where were you all,

That do yourselves the help of nature call,
Physicians? I acknowledce you were there
To sell such words as one in health would hear:
So died she. Curst be he who shall defend
Your art of hastening nature to its end!
In this you shewed that physic can but be
At best an art to cure your poverty.
Ye're many of you impostors, and do give
To sick men potions that yourselves may live.
He that hath surfeited, and cannot eat,
Must have a medicine to procure you meat;
And that's the deepest ground of all your skill,
Unless it be some knowledge how to kill.
Sorrow and madness make my verses flow
Cross to my understanding; for I know
You can do wonders: Every day I meet
The looser sort of people in the street
From desperate diseases freed; and why
Restore you them, and suffer her to die?
Why should the state allow you colleges,
Pensions for lectures, and anatomies,
If all your potions, vomits, letting blood,
Can only cure the bad, and not the good,
Which only they can do? and I will show
The hidden reason, why you did not know
The way to cure her: You believed her blood
Ran on such courses as you understood;
By lectures you believed her arteries
Grew as they do in your anatomies:
Forgetting that the state allows you none
But only whores and thieves to practise on
And every passage 'bout them I am sure
You understood, and only them can cure;
Which is the cause that both—
Are noted for enjoying so long lives.
But noble blood treads in too strange a path
For your ill-got experience, and hath
Another way of cure. If you had seen
Penelope dissected, or the Queen
Of Sheba; then you might have found a way
To have preserved her from that fatal day.
As 'tis, you have but made her sooner blest,
By sending her to Heaven, where let her rest.
I will not hurt the peace which she would have,
By longer looking in her quiet grave.

Upon the Silent Woman

Hear, you bad writers, and though you not see,
I will inform you where you happy be:
Provide the most malicious thoughts you can,
And bend them all against some private man,
To bring him, not his vices, on the stage;
Your envy shall be clad in some poor rage,
And your expressing of him shall be such,
That he himself shall think he hath no touch.
Where he that strongly writes, although he mean
To scourge but vices in a laboured scene,
Yet private faults shall be so well express'd
As men do get 'em, that each private breast,
That finds these errors in itself, shall say,
'He meant me, not my vices, in the play.'

A Funeral Elegy On the Death of The Lady Penelope Clifton

Since thou art dead, Clifton, the world may see
A certain end of flesh and blood in thee;
Till then a way was left for man to cry,
Flesh may be made so pure it cannot die;
But now thy unexpected death doth strike
With grief the better and the worse alike;
The good are sad they are not with thee there,
The bad have found they must not tarry here.
Death, I confess, 'tis just in thee to try
Thy pow'r on us, for thou thyself must die;
Thou pay'st but wages, Death, yet I would know
What strange delight thou tak'st to pay them so;
When thou com'st face to face thou strik'st us mute
And all our liberty is to dispute
With thee behind thy back, which I will use:
If thou hadst bravery in thee, thou wouldst choose
(Since thou art absolute, and canst controul
All things beneath a reasonable soul)
Some looked for way of killing; if her day
Had ended in a fire, a sword, or sea,
Or hadst thou come hid in a hundred years
To make an end of all her hopes and fears,
Or any other way direct to thee
Which Nature might esteem an enemy,
Who would have chid thee? now it shews thy hand
Desires to cozen where it might command:
Thou art not prone to kill, but where th' intent

Of those that suffer is their nourishment;
If thou canst steal into a dish, and creep
When all is still as though into a sleep,
And cover thy dry body with a draught,
Whereby some innocent lady may be caught,
And cheated of her life, then thou wilt come
And stretch thyself upon her early tomb,
And laugh as pleased, to show thou canst devour
Mortality as well by wit as pow'r.
I would thou hadst had eyes, or not a dart,
That yet at least, the clothing of that heart
Thou struck'st so spitefully might have appear'd
To thee, and with a reverence have been fear'd:
But since thou art so blind, receive from me
Who 'twas on whom thou wrought'st this tragedy;
She was a lady, who for public fame,
Never (since she in thy protection came,
Who sett'st all living tongues at large) received
A blemish; with her beauty she deceived
No man; when taken with it, they agree
'Twas Nature's fault, when from 'em 'twas in thee.
And such her virtue was, that although she
Received as much joy, having pass'd through thee,
As ever any did; yet hath thy hate
Made her as little better in her state,
As ever it did any being here;
She lived with us as if she had been there.
Such ladies thou canst kill no more, but so
I give thee warning here to kill no moe;
For if thou dost, my pen shall make the rest
Of those that live, especially the best,
Whom thou most thirstest for, to abandon all
Those fruitless things, which thou wouldst have us call
Preservatives, keeping, their diet so,
As the long-living poor their neighbours do:
Then shall we have them long, and they at last
Shall pass from thee to her, but not so fast.

The Examination of His Mistress's Perfections

Stand still my happiness, and swelling heart
No more, till I consider what thou art.
Desire of knowledge was man's fatal vice,
For when our parents were in paradise,
Though they themselves, and all they saw was good,
They thought it nothing if not understood;

And I (part of their seed struck with their sin)
Though by their bounteous favour I be in
A paradise where I may freely taste
Of all the virtuous pleasures which thou hast,
Wanting that knowledge, must in all my bliss
Err with my parents, and ask what it is.
My faith saith 'tis not Heaven, and I dare swear
If it be Hell no sense of pain is there;
Sure 'tis some pleasant place where I may stay,
As I to Heaven go in the middle way.
Wert thou but fair and no whit virtuous,
Thou wert no more to me but a fair house
Haunted with spirits, from which men do them bless,
And no man will half furnish to possess:
Or hadst thou worth wrapt in a rivell'd skin,
'Twere inaccessible; who durst go in
To find it out? far sooner would I go
To find a pearl covered witli hills of snow;
'Twere buried virtue, and thou mightst me move
To reverence the tomb, but not to love,
No more than dotingly to cast mine eye
Upon the urn where Luerece' ashes lie.
But thou art fair and sweet, and every good
That ever yet durst mix with flesh and blood:
The devil ne'er saw in his fallen state
An object whereupon to ground his hate
So fit as thee: all living things but he
Love thee; how happy then must that man be
Whom from amongst all creatures thou dost take?
Is there a hope beyond it? Can he make
A wish to change thee for? This is my bliss,
Let it run on now, I know what it is.

On the Marriage of a Beauteous Young Gentlewoman with An Ancient Man

Fondly, too curious Nature, to adorn
Aurora with the blushes of the morn:
Why do her rosy lips breath gums and spice;
Unto the East, and sweet to Paradise?
Why do her eyes open the day? her hand
And voice intrance the panther, and command
Incensed winds; her breasts, the tents of love,
Smooth as the godded swan, or Venus' dove;
Soft as the balmy dew whose every touch
Is pregnant; but why those rich spoils, when such
Wonder and perfection must be led

A bridal captive unto Tithon's bed?
Ag'd, and deformed Tithon! must thy twine
Circle and blast at once what care and time
Had made for wonder? must pure beauty have
No other foil but ruin and a grave?
So have I seen the pride of Nature's store,
The orient pearl chained to the sooty Moor;
So hath the diamond's bright ray been set
In night, and wedded to the negro jet.
See, see, how thick those showers of pearl do fall
To weep her ransom, or her funeral,
Whose every treasured drop, congealed, might bring,
Freedom and ransom to a fettered kin,
While tyrant Wealth stands by, and laughs to see
How he can wed love and antipathy.
Hymen, thy pine burns with adulterate fire;
Thou and thy quivered boy did once conspire
To mingle equal flames, and then no shine
Of gold, but beauty, dressed the Paphian shrine;
Roses and lilies kiss'd; the amorous vine
Did with the fair and straight-limb'd elm entwine.

Ad Comitissam Rutlandiæ

Madam, so may my verses pleasing be,
So may you laugh at them and not at me,
'Tis something to you gladly I would say;
But how to do't I cannot find the way.
I would avoid the common beaten ways
To women used, which are love or praise:
As for the first, the little wit I have
Is not yet grown so near unto the grave,
But that I can, by that dim fading light,
Perceive of what, or unto whom I write.
Let such as in a hopeless, witless rage,
Can sigh a quire, and read it to a page;
Such is do backs of books and windows fill,
With their too furious diamond or quill;
Such as were well resolved to end their days
With a loud laughter blown beyond the seas;
Who are so mortified that they can live
Contemned of all the world, and yet forgive,
Write love to you: I would not willingly
Be pointed at in every company;
As was that little tailor, who till death
Was hot in love with Queen Elizabeth:

And, for the last, in all my idle days
I never yet did living woman praise
In prose or verse: and when I do begin
I'll pick some woman out as full of sin
As you are full of virtue; with a soul
As black as you are white; a face as foul
As you are beautiful: for it shall be
Out of the rules of physiognomy
So far, that I do fear I must displace
The art a little, to let in her face.
It shall att least four faces be below
The devil's; and her parched corpse shall show
In her loose skill as if some sprite she were
Kept in a bag by some great conjurer.
Her breath shall be as horrible and wild
As every word you speak is sweet and mild;
It shall be such a one as will not be
Covered with any art or policy:
But let her take all powders, fumes, and drink,
She shall make nothing but a dearer stink;
She shall have such a foot and such a nose,
She shall not stand in anything but prose;
If I bestow my praises upon such,
'Tis charity, and I shall merit much.
My praise will come to her like a full bowl,
Bestowed at most need on a thirsty soul;
Where, if I sing your praises in my rhyme,
I lose my ink, my paper, and my time;
And nothing add to your o'erflowing store,
And tell you nought, but what you knew before.
Nor do the virtuous-minded (which I swear,
Madam, I think you are) endure to hear
Their own perfections into questions brought,
But stop their ears at them; for if I thought
You took a pride to have your virtues known,
Pardon me, madam, I should think them none.
To what a length is this strange letter grown,
In seeking of a subject, yet finds none!
But your brave thoughts, which I so much respect
Above your glorious titles, shall accept
These harsh disordered lines. I shall ere long
Dress up your virtues new, in a new song;
Yet far from all base praise and flattery,
Although I know whate'er my verses be,
They will like the most servile flattery shew,
If I write truth, and make the subject you.

An Elegy on the Lady Markham

As unthrifts groan in straw for their pawn'd beds,
As women weep for their lost maidenheads,
When both are without hope or remedy,
Such an untimely grief I have for thee.
I never saw thy face, nor did my heart
Urge forth mine eyes unto it whilst thou wert;
But being lifted hence, that, which to thee
Was death's sad dart, proved Cupid's shaft to me.
Whoever thinks me foolish that the force
Of a report can make me love a corse,
Know he that when with this I do compare
The love I do a living woman bear,
I find myself most happy: now I know
Where I can find my mistress, and can go
Unto her trimm'd bed, and can lift away
Her grass-green mantle, and her sheet display;
And touch her naked; and though th' envious mold
In which she lies uncover'd, moist, and cold,
Strive to corrupt her, she will not abide
With any art her blemishes to hide,
As many living do, and, know their need;
Yet cannot they in sweetness her exceed,
But make a stink with all their art and skill,
Which their physicians warrant with a bill;
Nor at her door doth heaps of coaches stay,
Footmen and midwives to bar up my way;
Nor needs she any maid or page to keep,
To knock me early from my golden sleep,
With letters that her honour all is gone,
If I not right her cause on such a one.
Her heart is not so hard to make me pay
For every kiss a supper and a play:
Nor will she ever open her pure lips
To utter oaths, enough to drown our ships,
To bring a plague, a famine, or the sword,
Upon the land, though she should keep her word;
Yet, ere an hour be past, in some new vein
Break them, and swear them double o'er again.
Pardon me, that with thy blest memory
I mingle mine own former misery:
Yet dare I not excuse the fate that brought
These crosses on me, for then every thought
That tended to thy love was black and foul,
Now all as pure as a new-baptiz'd soul:
For I protest, for all that I can see,

I would not lie one night in bed with thee;
Nor am I jealous, but could well abide
My foe to lie in quiet by thy side.
You worms, my rivals, whilst she was alive,
How many thousands were there that did strive
To have your freedom? for their sake forbear
Unseemly holes in her soft skin to wear:
But if you must (as what worms can abstain
To taste her tender body?) yet refrain
With your disordered eatings to deface her,
But feed yourselves so as you most may grace her.
First, through her ear-tips see you make a pair
Of holes, which, as the moist inclosed air
Turns into water, may the clean drops take,
And in her ears a pair of jewels make.
Have ye not yet enough of that white skin,
The touch whereof, in times past, would have been
Enough to have ransom'd many a thousand soul
Captive to love? If not, then upward roll
Your little bodies, where I would you have
This Epitaph upon her forehead grave:
'Living, she was young, fair, and full of wit;
Dead, all her faults are in her forehead writ.'

To The True Patronesse of All Poetrie

It is a statute in deepe wisdomes lore,
That for his lines none should a patron chuse
By wealth or pouerty, by lesse or more,
But who the same is able to peruse;
Nor ought a man his labours dedicate,
Without a true and sensible desert,
To any power of such a mighty state,
And such a wise Defendresse as thou art.
Thou great and powerfull Muse, then pardon mee,
That I presume the Mayden-cheeke to stayne,
In dedicating such a work to thee,
Sprung from the issue of an idle brayne.
I vse thee as a woman ought to be:
I consecrate my idle howres to thee.

Fie on Love

Now fie on foolish love, it not befits

Or man or woman know it.
Love was not meant for people in their wits,
And they that fondly show it
Betray the straw, and features in their brain,
And shall have Bedlam for their pain:
If simple love be such a curse,
To marry is to make it ten times worse.

To My Dear Friend M. Ben Jonson, On His Fox

If it might stand with justice to allow
The swift conversion of all follies; now,
Such is my mercy, that I could admit
All sorts should equally approve the wit
Of this thy even work, whose growing fame
Shall raise thee high, and thou it, with thy name.
And did not manners and my love command
Me to forbear to make those understand,
Whom thou, perhaps, hast in thy wiser doom
Long since firmly resolved, shall never come
To know more than they do; I would have shewn
To all the world, the art, which thou alone
Hast taught our tongue, the rules of time, of place,
And other rites, delivered, with the grace
Of comic style, which, only, is far more
Than any English stage hath known before.
But, since our subtle gallants think it good
To like of nought, that may be understood,
Lest they should he disproved; or have, at best,
Stomachs so raw, that nothing can digest
But what's obscene, or barks: let us desire
They may continue, simply, to admire
Fine clothes, and strange words; and may live, in age,
To see themselves ill brought upon the stage,
And like it: whilst thy bold and knowing muse
Contemns all praise, but such as thou wouldst choose.

To My Friend M. Ben Jonson, Upon His Catiline

If thou hadst itch'd after the wild applause
Of common people, and hadst made thy laws
In writing such as catch'd at present voice,
I should commend the thing, but not thy choice.
But thou hast squared thy rules by what is good,

And art three ages yet from understood:
And (I dare say) in it there lies much wit
Lost, till the reader can grow up to it;
Which they can ne'er outgrow, to find it ill,
But must fall back again, or like it still.

To My Friend Mr. John Fletcher, Upon His Faithful Sheperdess

I know too well, that, no more than the man,
That travels through the burning desarts, can,
When he is beaten with the raging sun,
Half-smother'd with the dust, have power to run
From a cool river, which himself doth find,
Ere he be slaked; no more can he, whose mind
Joys in the Muses hold from that delight,
When Nature and his full thoughts bid him write.
Yet wish I those, whom I for friends have known,
To sing their thoughts to no ears but their own.
Why should the man, whose wit ne'er had a stain,
Upon the public stage present his vein,
And make a thousand men in judgment sit,
To call in question his undoubted wit,
Scarce two of which can understand the laws
Which they should judge by, nor the, party's cause?
Among the rout, there is not one that hath
In his own censure an explicit faith;
One company, knowing they judgment lack,
Ground their belief onthe next man in black;
Others, on him that makes signs, and is mute;
Some like, as he does in the fairest suit;
He, as his mistress doth; and she, by chance;
Nor want there those, who, as the boy doth dance
Between the acts, will censure the whole play;
Some like if the wax-lights be new that day;
But multitudes there are, whose judgment goes
Headlong according to the actors' clothes.
For this, these public things and I agree
So ill, that, but to do a right to thee,
I had not been persuaded to have hurl'd
These few ill-spoken lines into the world;
Both to be read and censured of by those
Whose very reading makes verse senseless prose;
Such as must spend above an hour to spell
A challenge on a post, to know it well.
But since it was thy hap to throw away
Much wit, for which the people did not pay,

Because they saw it not, I not dislike
This second publication, which may strike
Their conisciences, to see the thing they scorn'd,
To he with so much wit and art adorn'd.
Besides, one 'vantage more in this I see,
Your censurers must have the quality
Of reading, which I am afraid is more
Than half your shrewdest judges had before.

The Remedy of Love

When Cupid read this title, straight he said,
'Wars, I perceive, against me will be made.'
But spare, oh Love! to tax thy poet so,
Who oft bath borne thy ensign 'gainst thy foe;
I am not he by whom thy mother bled,
When she to heaven on Mars his horses fled.
I oft, like other youths, thy flame did prove,
And if thou ask, what I do still? I love.
Nay, I have taught by art to keep Love's course,
And made that reason which before was force.
I seek not to betray thee, pretty boy,
Nor what I once have written to destroy.
If any love, and find his mistress kind,
Let him go on, and sail with his own wind;
But he that by his love is discontented,
To save his life my verses were invented.
Why should a lover kill himself? or why
Should any, with his own grief wounded, die?
Thou art a boy, to play becomes thee still,
Thy reign is soft; play then, and do not kill;
Or if thou'lt needs be vexing, then do this,
Make lovers meet by stealth, and steal a kiss
Make them to fear lest any overwatch them,
And tremble when they think some come to catch them;
And with those tears that lovers shed all night,
Be thou content, but do not kill outright.—
Love heard, and up his silver wings did heave,
And said, 'Write on; I freely give thee leave.'
Come then, all ye despised, that love endure,
I, that have felt the wounds, your love will cure;
But come at first, for if you make delay,
Your sickness will grow mortal by your stay:
The tree, which by delay is grown so big,
In the beginning was a tender twig;
That which at first was but a span in length,

Will, by delay, be rooted past men's strength.
Resist beginnings, medicines bring no curing
Where sickness is grown strong by long enduring.
When first thou seest a lass that likes thine eye,
Bend all thy present powers to descry
Whether her eye or carriage first would shew
If she be fit for love's delights or no:
Some will be easy, such an one elect;
But she that bears too grave and stern aspect,
Take heed of her, and make her not thy jewel,
Either she cannot love, or will be cruel.
If love assail thee there, betime take heed,
Those wounds are dangerous that inward bleed;
He that to-day cannot shake off love's sorrow,
Will certainly be more unapt to-morrow.
Love bath so eloquent and quick a tongue,
That he will lead thee all thy life along,
And on a sudden clasp thee in a yoke,
Where thou must either draw, or striving choke.
Strive then betimes, for at the first one hand
May stop a water-drill that wears the sand
But, if delayed, it breaks into a flood,
Mountains will hardly make the passage good.
But I am out, for now I do begin
To keep them off, not heal those that are in.
First, therefore, lovers, I intend to shew
How love came to you, then how he may go.
You that would not know what love's passions be,
Never be idle, learn that rule of me.
Ease makes you love, as that o'ercomes your wills,
Ease is the food and cause of all your ills.
Turn ease and idleness but out of door,
Love's darts are broke, his flame can burn no more.
As feeds and willows love the water's side,
So love loves with the idle to abide.
If then at liberty you fain would be,
Love yields to labour, labour and be free.
Long sleeps, soft beds, rich vintage, and high feeding,
Nothing to do, and pleasure of exceeding,
Dulls all our senses, makes our virtue stupid,
And then creeps in that crafty villain Cupid.
That boy loves ease a' life, hates such a stir,
Therefore thy mind to better things prefer.
Behold thy country's enemies in arms,
At home love gripes the heart in his sly charms;
Then rise and put on armour, cast off sloth,
Thy labour may at once o'ercome them both!
If this seem hard and too unpleasant, then

Behold the law set forth by God and men;
Sit down and study that, that thou may'st know
The way to guide thyself, and others shew.
Or if thou lov'st not to be shut up so,
Learn to assail the deer with trusty bow,
That through the woods thy well-mouth'd bounds may ring,
Whose echo better joys than love will sing:
There may'st thou chance to bring thy love to end;
Diana unto Venus is no friend.
The country will afford thee means enow,
Sometimes disdain not to direct the plough;
To follow through the fields the bleating lamb,
That mourns to miss the comfort of his dam.
Assist the harvest, help to prune the trees,
Graft, plant, and sow, no kind of labour leese.
Set nets for birds, with hook'd lines bait for fish,
Which will employ thy mind and fill thy dish;
That, being weary with these pains, at night
Sound sleep may put the thoughts of love to flight.
With such delights, or labours as are these,
Forget to love, and learn thyself to please.
But chiefly learn this lesson, for my sake,
Fly from her far, some journey undertake:
I know thou'lt grieve, and that her name once told,
Will be enough thy journey to withhold;
But when thou find'st thyself most bent to stay,
Compel thy feet to run with thee away.
Nor do thou wish that rain or stormy weather
May stay your steps, and bring you back together;
Count not the miles you pass, nor doubt the way,
Lest those respects should turn you back to stay.
Tell not the clock, nor look not once behind,
But fly like lightning, or the northern wind:
For, where we are too much o'ermatch'd in might,
There is no way for safe-guard but by flight.
But some will count my lines too hard and bitter:
I must confess them hard; but yet 'tis better
To fast a while, that health may be provoked,
Than feed at plenteous tables and be choked.
To cure the wretched body, I am sure
Both fire and steel thou gladly wilt endure:
Wilt thou not then take pains by any art
To cure thy mind, which is thy better part?
The hardness is at first, and that once past,
Pleasant and easy ways will come at last.
I do not bid thee strive with witches' charms,
Or such unholy acts, to cure thy harms;
Ceres herself, who all these things did know,

Had never power to cure her own love so:
No, take this medicine, (which of all is sure)
Labour and absence is the only cure.
But if the fates compel thee in such fashion,
That thou must needs live near her habitation,
And canst not fly her sight, learn here of me,
Thou that would'st fain, and canst, not yet be free:
Set all thy mistress' faults before thine eyes,
And all thy own disgraces well advise;
Say to thyself, that 'she is covetous,
Hath ta'en my gifts, and used me thus and thus;
Thus hath she sworn to me, and thug deceived;
Thus have I hoped, and thus have been bereaved.
With love she feeds my rival, while I starve,
And pours on him kisses which I deserve:
She follows him with smiles, and gives to me
Sad looks; no lover's, but a stranger's fee.
All those embraces I so oft desired,
To him she offers daily unrequired;
Whose whole desert, and half mine weighed together,
Would make mine lead, and his seem cork and feather;
Then let her go, and, since she proves so hard,
Regard thyself, and give her no regard.'
Thus must thou school thyself, and I could wish
Thee to thyself most eloquent in this.
But put on grief enough, and do not fear,
Grief will enforce thy eloquence t' appear.
Thus I myself the love did once expel
Of one whose coyness vex'd my soul like hell.
I must confess she touch'd me to the quick,
And 1, that am physician, then was sick;
But this I found to profit: I did still
Ruminate what I thought in her was ill;
And, for to cure myself, I found a way,
Some honest slanders on her for to lay
Quoth I, 'How lamely doth my mistress go!'
(Although I must confess it was not so;)
I said her arms were crooked, fingers bent,
Her shoulders bow'd, her legs consumed and spent;
Her colour sad, her neck as dark as night,
When Venus might in all have ta'en delight.
But yet, because I would no more come nigh her,
Myself unto myself did thus bely her.
Do thou the like, and, though she fair appear,
Think vice to virtue often comes too near;
And in that error (though it be an error)
Preserve thyself from any further terror.
If she be round and plump, say she's too fat;

If brown, say black, and thick, who cares for that?
If she be slender, swear she is too lean,
That such a wench will wear a man out clean.
If she be red, say she's too full of blood;
If pale, her body nor her mind is good;
If wanton, say, she seeks thee to devour;
If grave, neglect her, say, she looks too sour.
Nay, if she have a fault, and thou do'st know it,
Praise it, that in thy presence she may show it:
As, if her voice be bad, crack'd in the ring,
Never give over till thou make her sing;
If she have any blemish in her foot,
Commend her dancing still, and put her to't;
If she be rude of speech, incite her talk;
If halting lame, provoke her much to walk;
Or if on instruments she have small skill,
Reach down a viol, urge her to that still;
Take any way to ease thy own distress,
And think those faults be which are nothing less.
Then meditate besides what thing it is
That makes thee still in love to go amiss.
Advise thee well, for as the world now goes,
Men are not caught with substance but with shows.
Women are in their bodies turn'd to French,
That face and body's least part of a wench.
I know a woman hath in love been troubled
For that which tailors make, a find neat doublet;
And men are even as mad in their desiring,
That oftentimes love women for their tiring:
He that doth so, let him take this advice:
Let him rise early, and not being nice,
Up to his mistress' chamber let him hie
Ere she arise, and there he shall espy
Such a confusion of disordered things,
In boddice, jewels, tires, wires, lawns, and rings,
That sure it cannot choose but much abhor him,
To see her lie in pieces thus before him;
And find those things shut in a painted box,
For which he loves her and endures her mocks.
Once I myself had a great mind to see
What kind of things women undressed be;
And found my sweetheart, just when I came at her,
Screwing her teeth, and dipping rags in water.
She missed her perriwig, and durst not stay,
But put it on in haste the backward way;
That, had I not o' th' sudden changed my mind,
I had mistook and kiss'd my love behind:
So, if thou wish her faults should rid thy cares,

Watch out thy time, and take her unawares;
Or rather put the better way in proof,
Come thou not near, but keep thyself aloof.
If all this serve not, use one medicine more,
Seek out another love, and her adore.
But choose out one in whom thou wed may'st see
A heart inclined to love and cherish thee:
For, as a river parted slower goes,
So love, thus parted, still more evenly flows.
One anchor will not serve a vessel tall,
Nor is one hook enough to fish withall;
He that can solace him and sport with two,
May in the end triumph as others do.
Thou, that to one hast shewed thyself too kind,
May'st in a second much more comfort find;
If one love entertain thee with despite,
The other will embrace thee with delight;
When by the former thou art made accurst,
The second will contend to excel the first,
And strive with love to drive her from thy breast:
That first to second yields, women know best.
Or if to yield to either thou art loth,
This may perhaps acquit thee of them both;
For what one love makes odd, two shall make even;
Thus blows with blows, and fire with fire's out driven.
Perchance this course win turn thy first love's heart,
And when thine is at ease, cause her's to smart,
If thy love's rival stick so near thy side,
Think, women can copartners worse abide;
For though thy mistress never means to love thee,
Yet from the other's love she'll strive to move thee:
But let her strive, she oft hath vex'd thy heart,
Suffer her now to bear herself a part;
And though thy bowels burn like Ætna's fire,
Seem colder far than ice, or her desire;
Feign thyself free, and sigh not overmuch,
But laugh aloud when grief thy heart doth touch.
I do not bid thee break through fire and flame,
Such violence in love is much to blame;
But I advise that thou dissemble deep,
And all thy passions in thine own breast keep.
Feign thyself well, and thou at last shalt see
Thyself as well'as thou didst feign to be:
So have I often, when I would not drink,
Sat down as one asleep, and feign'd to wink,
Till, as I nodding sat, and took no heed,
I have at last fall'n fast asleep indeed;
So have I oft been angry, feigning spite,

And, counterfeiting smiles, have laughed outright;
So love by use doth come, by use doth go,
And he that feigns well shall at length be so.
If e'er thy mistress promised to receive thee
Into her bosom, and did then deceive thee,
Locking thy rival in, thee out of door,
Be not dejected, seem not to deplore,
Nor when thou seest her next take notice of it,
But pass it over, it shall turn to profit:
For if she sees such tricks, as these perplex thee,
She will be proud, and take delight to vex thee,
But if she prove thee constant in this kind,
She will begin at length some sleights to find,
How she may draw thee back, and keep thee still
A servile captive to her fickle will.
But now take heed, here comes the proof of men,
Be thou as constant as thou seemest then:
Receive no messages, regard no lines,
They are but snares to catch thee in her twines;
Receive no gifts, think all that praise her flatter;
Whate'er she writes believe not half the matter.
Converse not with her servant, nor her maid,
Scarce bid good-morrow, lest thou be betray'd.
When thou goest by her door never look back,
And though she call do not thy journey slack.
If she should send her friends to talk with thee,
Suffer them not too long to walk with thee;
Do not believe one word they say is sooth,
Nor do not ask so much as how she doth;
Yea, though thy very heart should burn to know,
Bridle thy tongue, and make thereof no show:
Thy careless silence shall perplex her more
Than can a thousand sighs sigh'd o'er and o'er.
By saying, thou lovest not, thy loving prove not,
For he's far gone in love, that says, 'I love not:'
Then hold thy peace, and shortly love will die,
That wound heals best, that cures not by and by.
But some will say, 'Alas, this rule is hard!
Must we not love where we may find reward?
How should a tender woman bear this scorn,
That cannot, without art, by men be borne?'
Mistake me not; I do not wish you show
Such a contempt to them whose love you know;
But where a scornful lass makes you endure
Her slight regarding, there I lay my cure.
Nor think in leaving love you wrong your lass,
Who one to her content already has;
While she doth joy in him, joy thou in any,

Thou hast, as well as she, the choice of many:
Then, for thy own contempt, defer not long,
But cure thyself, and she shall have no wrong.
Among all cures I chiefly do commend
Absence in this to be the only friend;
And so it is, but I would have ye learn
The perfect use of absence to discern.
First then, when thou art absent to her sight,
In solitariness do not delight:
Be seldom left alone, for then I know
A thousand vexing thoughts will come and go.
Fly lonely walks, and uncouth places sad,
They are the nurse of thoughts that make men mad.
Walk not too much where thy fond eye may see
The place where she did give love's rights to thee:
For even the place will tell thee of those joys,
And turn thy kisses into sad annoys.
Frequent not woods and groves, nor sit and muse
With arms across, as foolish lovers use;
For as thou sitt'st alone thou soon shalt find
Thy mistress' face presented to thy mind,
As plainly to thy troubled phantasy,
As if she were in presence, and stood by.
This to eschew open thy doors all day,
Shun no man's speech that comes into thy way;
Admit all companies, and when there's none,
Then walk thou forth thyself, and seek out one;
When he is found, seek more, laugh, drink, and sing;
Rather than be alone do anything.
Or if thou be constrained to be alone,
Have not her picture for to gaze upon:
For that's the way, when thou art eased of pain,
To wound anew and make thee sick again;
Or if thou hast it, think the painter's skill
Flattered her face, and that she looks more ill;
And think, as thou dost musing on it sit,
That she herself is counterfeit like it:
Or rather fly all things that are inclined
To bring one thought of her into thy mind;
View not her tokens, nor think on her words,
But take some book, whose learned womb affords
Physic for souls, there search for some relief
To 'guile the time, and rid away thy grief.
But if thy thoughts on her must needs be bent,
Think what a deal of precious time was spent
In quest of her; and that thy best of youth
Languish'd and died while she was void of truth;
Think but how ill she did deserve affection,

And yet how long she held thee in subjection;
Think how she changed, how ill it did become her,
And thinking so, leave love, and fly far from her.
He that from all infection would be free,
Must fly the place where the infected be:
And he that would from love's affection fly,
Must leave his mistress' walks, and not come nigh.
Sore eyes are got by looking on sore eyes,
And wounds do soon from new-heal'd sears arise;
As embers touch'd with sulphur do renew,
So will her sight kindle fresh flames in you.
If then thou meet'st her, suffer her go by thee,
And be afraid to let her come too nigh thee
For her aspect will cause desire in thee,
And hungry men scarce hold from meat, they see.
If e'er she sent thee letters, that lie by,
Peruse them not, they'll captivate thy eye,
But lap them up, and cast them in the fire,
And wish, as they waste, so may thy desire.
If e'er thou sent'st her token, gift, or letter,
Go not to fetch them back; for it is better
That she detain a little paltry pelf,
Than thou should'st seek for them and lose thyself
For why? her sight will so enchant thy heart
That thou wilt lose thy labour, I my art.
But if, by chance, there fortune such a case,
Thou needs must come where she shall be in place,
Then call to mind all parts of this discourse,
For sure thou shalt have need of an thy force.
Against thou goest curl not thy head and hair,
Nor care whether thy band be foul or fair;
Nor be not in so neat and spruce array
As if thou mean'st to make it holiday;
Neglect thyself for once, that she may see
Her love hath now no power to work on thee;
And if thy rival be in presence too,
Seem not to mark, but do as others do;
Salute him friendly, give him gentle words,
Return all courtesies that he affords:
Drink to him, carve him, give him compliment;
This shall thy mistress more than thee torment:
For she will think, by this thy careless show,
Thou car'st not now whether she love or no.
But if thou canst persuade thyself indeed
She bath no lover, but of thee hath need,
That no man loves her but thyself alone,
And that she shall be lost when thou art gone;
Thus sooth thyself, and thou shalt seem to be

In far more happy taking than is she.
For if thou think'st she's loved and loves again,
Hell-fire will seem more easy than thy pain.
But chiefly when in presence thou shalt spy
The man she most affecteth standing by,
And see him grasp her by the tender hand,
And whispering close, or almost kissing stand;
When thou shalt doubt whether they laugh at thee,
Or whether on some meeting they agree;
If now thou canst hold out, thou art a man,
And canst perform more than thy teacher can;
If then thy heart can be at ease and free,
I will give o'er to teach, and learn of thee.
But this way I would take: among them all,
I would pick out some lass to talk withall,
Whose, quick inventions and whose nimble wit
Should busy mine and keep me from my fit:
My eye with all my heart should be a-wooing,
No matter what I said so I were doing;
For all that while my love should think at least
That I, as well as she, on love did feast;
And though my heart were thinking of her face,
Of her unkindness and my own disgrace,
Of all my present pains by her neglect,
Yet would I laugh, and seem without respect.
Perchance, in envy thou should'st sport with any,
Her beck will single thee from forth of many:
But, if thou canst, of all that present are,
Her conference alone thou should'st forbear;
For if her looks so much thy mind do trouble,
Her honied speeches will distract thee double.
If she begin once to confer with thee,
Then do as I would do, be ruled by me:
When she begins to talk, imagine straight,
That now to catch thee up she lies in wait;
Then call to mind some business or affair,
Whose doubtful issue takes up all thy care;
That while such talk thy troubled fancies stirs,
Thy mind may work, and give no heed to her's.
Alas! I know men's hearts, and that full soon,
By women's gentle words we are undone;
If women sigh or weep, our souls are grieved,
Or if they swear they love, they are believed.
But trust not thou to oaths if she should swear,
Nor hearty sighs, believe they dwell not there.
If she should grieve in earnest or in jest,
Or force her arguments with sad protest,
As if true sorrow in her eyelid sate,

Nay, if she come to weeping, trust not that;
For know that women can both weep and smile,
With much more danger than the crocodile.
Think all she doth is but to breed thy pain,
And get the power to tyrannize again;
And she will beat thy heart with trouble more
Than rocks are beat with waves tipon the shore.
Do not complain to her then of thy wrong,
But lock thy thoughts within thy silent tongue,
Tell her not why thou leav'st her, nor declare
(Although she ask thee) what thy torments are.
Wring not her fingers, gaze not on her eye;
From thence a thousand snares and arrows fly:
No, let her not perceive, by sighs and signs,
How at her deeds thy inward soul repines.
Seem careless of her speech, and do not hark,
Answer by chance as though thou didst not mark;
And if she bid thee home, straight promise not,
Or break thy word as if thou hadst forgot;
Seem not to care whether thou come or no,
And if she be not earnest do not go;
Feign thou hast business, and defer the meeting,
As one that greatly cared not for her greeting,
And as she talks cast thou thine eyes elsewhere,
And look among the lasses that are there;
Compare their several beauties to her face,
Some one or other will her form disgrace;
On both their faces carry still thy view,
Balance them equally in judgment true:
And when thou find'st the other doth excel
(Yet that thou canst not love it half so well)
Blush that thy passions make thee dote on her
More than on those thy judgment doth prefer.
When thou hast let her speak all that she would,
Seem as thou hast not one word understood:
And when to part with thee thou see'st her bent,
Give her some ordinary compliment,
Such as may seem of courtesy, not love,
And so to other company remove.
This carelessness, in which thou seem'st to be,
(Howe'er in her) will work this change in thee,
That thou shalt think, for using her so slight,
She cannot choose but turn her love to spite:
And if thou art persuaded once she hates,
Thou wilt beware, and not come near her baits.
But though I wish thee constantly believe
She hates thy sight, thy passions to deceive;
Yet be not thou so base to hate her too,

That which seems ill in her do not thou do;
'Twill indiscretion seem, and want of wit,
Where thou didst love to hate instead of it;
And thou may'st shame ever to be so mated,
And joined in love with one that should be hated:
Such kind of love is fit for clowns and hinds,
And not for debonair and gentle minds;
For can there be in man a madness more
Than hate those lips he wish'd to kiss before,
Or loath to see those eyes, or hear that voice
Whose very sound bath made his heart rejoice?
Such acts as these much indiscretion shews,
When men from kissing turn to wish for blows:
And this their own example shews so naught,
That when they should direct they must be taught:
But thou wilt say, 'For all the love I bear her,
And all the service, I am ne'er the nearer;'
And, which thee most of all doth vex like hell,
'She loves a man ne'er loved her half so well:
Him she adores, but I must not come at her,
Have I not then good reason for to hate her?'
I answer, no; for make the cause thine own,
And in thy glass her actions shall be shown:
When thou thyself in love wert so far gone,
Say, couldst thou love any but her alone?
I know thou could'st not, though with tears and cries
These had made deaf thine ears, and dim thine eyes:
Would'st thou for this that they hate thee again?
If so thou would'st, then hate thy love again:
Your faults are both alike; thou lovest her,
And she in love thy rival doth prefer:
If then her love to him thy hate procure,
Thou should'st for loving her like hate endure:
Then do not hate; for all the lines I write
Are not address'd to turn thy love to spite,
But writ to draw thy doting mind from love,
That in the golden mean thy thoughts may move;
In which, when once thou find'st thyself at quiet,
Learn to preserve thyself with this good diet.

FRANCIS BEAUMONT – A SHORT BIOGRAPHY

Francis Beaumont was born in 1584 near the small Leicestershire village of Thringstone. Unfortunately precise records of much of his short life do not exist.

He was the son to Sir Francis Beaumont of Grace Dieu, a justice of the common pleas. His mother was Anne, the daughter of Sir George Pierrepont.

The first date we can give for his education is at age 13 when he begins at Broadgates Hall (now Pembroke College, Oxford). Sadly, his father died the following year, 1598. Beaumont left university without a degree and entered the Inner Temple in London in 1600. A career choice of Law taken previously by his father.

The information to hand is confident that Beaumont's career in law was short-lived. He was quickly attracted to the theatre and soon became first an admirer and then a student of poet and playwright Ben Jonson. Jonson at this time was a cultural behemoth; very talented and a life full of volatility that included frequent brushes with the authorities. His followers, including the poet Robert Herrick, were known as 'the sons of Ben'. Beaumont was also on friendly terms with other luminaries such as the poet Michael Drayton.

Beaumont's first work was Salmacis and Hermaphroditus, it debuted in 1602. A 1911 edition of the Encyclopædia Britannica includes the description "not on the whole discreditable to a lad of eighteen, fresh from the popular love-poems of Marlowe and Shakespeare, which it naturally exceeds in long-winded and fantastic diffusion of episodes and conceits."

By 1605, Beaumont had written commendatory verses to Volpone one of Ben Jonson's masterpieces.

It was now, in the early years of the 17th Century, that he met John Fletcher and together they gradually formed one of the most dynamic and productive of writing teams that English theatre has ever produced.

Their playwriting careers at this stage were both troubled by early failure. Beaumont had written The Knight of the Burning Pestle and it was first performed by the Children of the Blackfriars company in 1607. The audience however was distinctly unimpressed. The publisher's epistle in the 1613 quarto says they failed to note "the privie mark of irony about it."

The following year, Fletcher's Faithful Shepherdess failed on the same stage.

In 1609, however, the two collaborated in earnest on Philaster. The play was performed by the King's Men at the Globe Theatre and at Blackfriars. It was a great success. Their careers were now well and truly launched and into the bargain they had ignited and captured a public taste for tragicomedy.

There is an account that at the time the two men shared everything. They lived together in a house on the Bankside in Southwark, "they also lived together in Bankside, sharing clothes and having one wench in the house between them." Or as another account puts it "sharing everything in the closest intimacy."

This arrangement stopped in about 1613 when Beaumont married Ursula Isley, daughter and co-heiress of Henry Isley of Sundridge in Kent, by whom he had two daughters (one of them was born after his death).

Beaumont, at a very young age even for those times, was struck down by a stroke at some point in mid-1613, after which he was unable to write any more plays, but he did manage to write an elegy for Lady Penelope Clifton, who had died on 26th October 1613.

Francis Beaumont died on March 6th, 1616 and was buried in Westminster Abbey.

In his short life his canon was small but influential. Although he is seen more as a dramatist his poetry was celebrated even then and it continues to gain an avid readership to this day.

It was said at one point of the collaboration of Beaumont and Fletcher that "in their joint plays their talents are so ... completely merged into one, that the hand of Beaumont cannot clearly be distinguished from that of Fletcher." Whilst it was the view then it has not endured into modern times. Indeed, slowly but with certainty the name of Beaumont has been removed from many of their joint works. It has given way to other such luminaries as Philip Massinger, Nathan field and James Shirley.

FRANCIS BEUMONT – A CONCISE BIBLIOGRAPHY

This bibliography gives the most likely date of writing together with when published, revised or licensed by the Master or the Revels (This position within the royal household was originally for royal festivities, ie revels, and later to oversee stage censorship, until this function was transferred to the Lord Chamberlain in 1624).

Francis Beaumont – Solo Plays
The Knight of the Burning Pestle, comedy (performed 1607; printed 1613)
The Masque of the Inner Temple and Gray's Inn, masque (printed 1613)

Francis Beaumont & John Fletcher
The Woman Hater, comedy (1606; 1607)
Cupid's Revenge, tragedy (c. 1607–12; 1615)
Philaster, or Love Lies a-Bleeding, tragicomedy (c. 1609; 1620)
The Maid's Tragedy, Tragedy (c. 1609; 1619)
A King and No King, tragicomedy (1611; 1619)
The Captain, comedy (c. 1609–12; 1647)
The Scornful Lady, comedy (c. 1613; 1616)
Love's Pilgrimage, tragicomedy (c. 1615–16; 1647)
The Noble Gentleman, comedy (c. 1613; licensed 3 February 1626; 1647)

Francis Beaumont with John Fletcher & Philip Massinger
Thierry & Theodoret, tragedy (c. 1607; 1621)
The Coxcomb, comedy (c. 1608–10; 1647)
Beggars' Bush, comedy (c. 1612–13; revised 1622; 1647)
Love's Cure, comedy (c. 1612–13; revised 1625; 1647)

www.ingramcontent.com/pod-product-compliance
Lightning Source LLC
Chambersburg PA
CBHW060055050426
42448CB00011B/2472